Early Literacy Skills

Projects and Activities for Grades K-3

Written by Denise Bieniek

Illustrated by Laura Ferraro

Troll Early Learning Activities

Troll Early Learning Activities is a classroom-tested series designed to provide time-pressured teachers with a wide range of theme-related projects and activities to enhance lesson plans and enrich the curriculum. Each book focuses on a different area of early childhood learning, from math and writing to art and science. Using a wide range of activities, each title in this series is chockful of innovative ideas, handy reproducible pages, puzzles and games, classroom projects, suggestions for bulletin boards and learning centers, and much more.

With highly interactive student projects and teacher suggestions that make learning fun, Troll Early Learning Activities is an invaluable classroom resource you'll turn to again and again. We hope you will enjoy using the worksheets and activities presented in these books. And we know your students will benefit from the dynamic, creative learning environment you have created!

Titles in this series:

Animal Friends: Projects and Activities for Grades K-3

Circle Time Fun: Projects and Activities for Grades Pre-K-2

Classroom Decorations: Ideas for a Creative Classroom

Early Literacy Skills: Projects and Activities for Grades K-3

Helping Hands: Small Motor Skills Projects and Activities

Hi, Neighbor! Projects and Activities About Our Community

Number Skills: Math Projects and Activities for Grades K-3

People of the World: Multicultural Projects and Activities

Our World: Science Projects and Activities for Grades K-3

Seasons and Holidays: Celebrations All Year Long

Story Time: Skill-Building Projects and Activities for Grades K-3

Time, Money, Measurement: Projects and Activities Across the Curriculum

Metric Conversion Chart

1 inch = 2.54 cm	1 foot = .305 m	1 yard = .914 m
1 mile = 1.61 km	1 fluid ounce = 29.573 ml	1 cup = .24 l
1 pint = .473 l	1 teaspoon = 4.93 ml	1 tablespoon = 14.78 ml

Contents

Setting Up a Listening Center

Materials:

- table and chairs
- rug, pillows or cushions, stuffed animals
- construction paper
- markers
- scissors
- cassette recorder
- headphones and headphone jacks
- books and matching story cassettes
- large see-through freezer bags
- adhesive tape
- hole puncher
- hooks

LISTENING CENTER INSTRUCTIONS:
1. Select a story and its tape.
2. Listen to the tape while reading along in the book.
3. When finished, be sure to return the book and tape to their correct bag and hook on the wall.

Directions:

1. Place a table in a quiet area of the classroom. Try to furnish the area with chairs, a rug, soft pillows or cushions, and some stuffed animals.

2. Use construction paper, markers, and scissors to make decorations for the area. Provide a poster that gives students instructions on how to use the listening center. Instructions may include how to use the cassette recorder, the sequence of listening to a story (beginning with selecting a book and its cassette and ending with putting them away in the right place), and how to run the recorder.

3. Try to connect two or more headphones to the recorder. This will help cut down considerably on noise.

4. Place books and their cassettes in large see-through freezer bags so students can see the choices. Place a 3" piece of strong adhesive tape across the top of each bag. Then punch a hole in the middle of the tape so that each bag can be hung.

5. Attach hooks from which to hang the bags to a nearby wall or on the side of a cabinet.

Our Journals

Sept. 8

Today was the first day of school.

I have a new lunch box. I like my teacher. Her name is Miss Evans.

4. Tell students that they should try to write a word even if they are not sure of the exact spelling. Inventive spelling helps children write more easily and freely. If desired, students can recheck their spellings later, making corrections when needed. You may also wish to have students create their own dictionaries (or a class dictionary), following the directions on page 49.

5. Review each child's journal periodically. Share the journals with parents during school conferences to show how their children are progressing with their language skills.

February 18

Yesterday we gave a performance in my ballet class.

Mom and Dad came to see me dance. We wore pink tutus.

1. Help young children develop a love of writing by creating whole language journals to use throughout the school year. Begin by sending a note home asking that each student bring in a large composition book.

2. Then hold a class discussion about keeping a journal. Explain to students that a journal is a record of the things they have done during a certain period of time. Tell the children that it is often fun to look back at a journal and think about our experiences and adventures.

3. Encourage students to write in their journals and to illustrate their thoughts. For young children who are just learning their letters, help them write a short sentence or two about each illustration. For those children learning beginning sounds, ask them to write the beginning letter of each word in their thoughts. Later, have students "read" their thoughts back to you. As the year progresses, students will begin to add ending and middle sounds, and write out simple words in their entirety. You might also suggest certain activities for students to include in their journals, for example, poems, short stories, and other creative writing assignments.

Rhyme Time

Play these games with students to reinforce rhyming skills.

Materials:

- 5" x 7" index cards
- markers
- file box

Directions:

1. Write these suggested rhymes on index cards:

One, two,
buckle my shoe.

Rain, rain, go away!
Come again another day.

Little Miss Muffet
sat on a tuffet.

Jack and Jill
went up the hill.

Hickory, dickory, dock,
the mouse ran up the clock.

2. Read the poems to the class, and ask them to listen for the rhyming words in each verse. When each rhyme has been read, ask a volunteer to name the rhyming pairs.

3. Encourage students to write their own rhyming couplets. For example, "I went to the park when it was dark." Write these poems on index cards and place them in a file box. Make a label for the file box that says, "Rhyme Time."

Materials:

- various small toys and objects that rhyme (i.e., car/star or fish/dish)
- small plastic containers
- medium-sized cardboard box

Directions:

1. Place the objects in a medium-sized cardboard box with small plastic containers nearby.

2. Ask students to name each object, then place it in a container with its rhyming match.

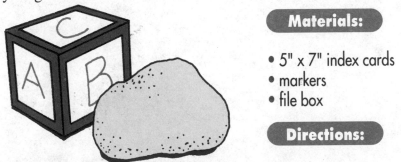

Materials:

- 5" x 7" index cards
- markers
- file box

Directions:

1. Write the following suggested riddles on index cards:

I rhyme with store. You open and shut me. What am I? (a door)
I rhyme with pool. You sit on me. What am I? (a stool)
I rhyme with block. You find me outdoors. What am I? (a rock)
I rhyme with sneeze. You say this to be polite. What am I? (please)

2. Read the riddles to the class, and ask them to listen for the clues to the answers. When each riddle has been read, ask a student to say the answer.

3. Encourage students to write their own rhyming riddles. Write the riddles on index cards, and place them in a file box. Label the file box, "Riddle Me This!"

Because I Said So! Listening Game

1. Gather the class together in a large, empty space. Explain that you will be giving them some directions to follow. The directions may or may not be silly, but students will have to do them to show that they are listening.

2. Some directions to begin the game:

Touch your toes.

Reach for the stars.

Hop like a kangaroo.

Touch your hair and run in place.

3. Progress to more challenging directions as the students' ability to follow increases.

Shake hands with the person next to you and make a sad face.

Walk three paces, turn around, then hold up a hand.

Flap your arms, roll your eyes, stamp your foot, and clap your hands.

4. Since the object of this game is to get students to practice their listening skills, be sure to give the directions only once.

I See the Sea Homonyms Game

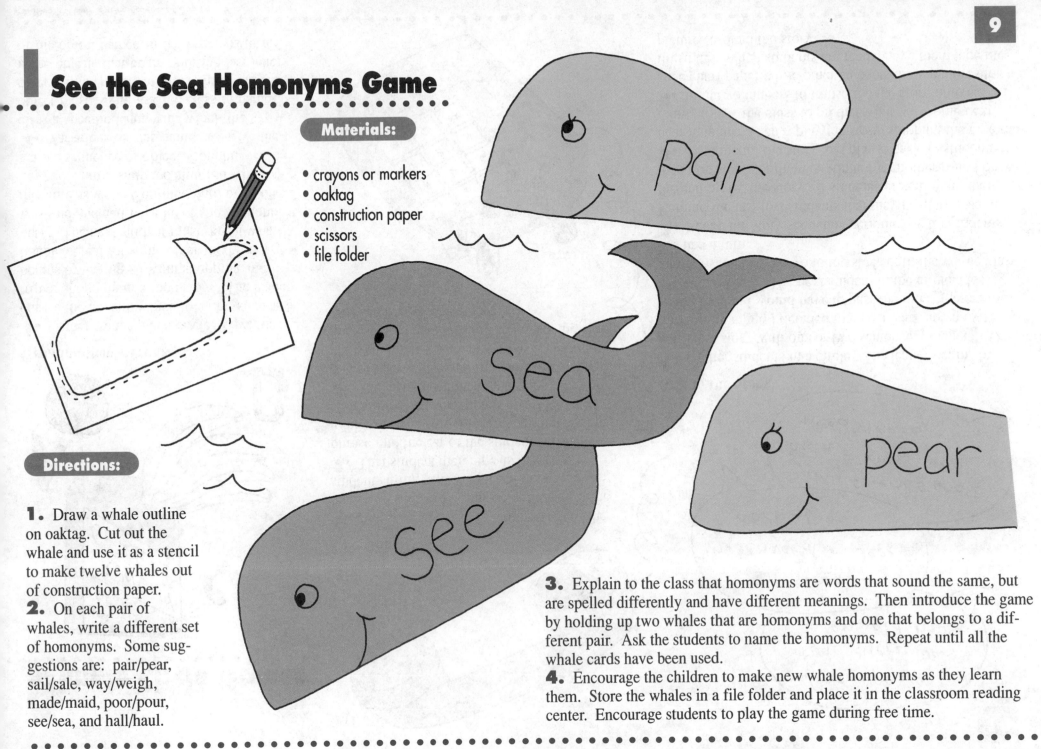

Materials:

- crayons or markers
- oaktag
- construction paper
- scissors
- file folder

Directions:

1. Draw a whale outline on oaktag. Cut out the whale and use it as a stencil to make twelve whales out of construction paper.

2. On each pair of whales, write a different set of homonyms. Some suggestions are: pair/pear, sail/sale, way/weigh, made/maid, poor/pour, see/sea, and hall/haul.

3. Explain to the class that homonyms are words that sound the same, but are spelled differently and have different meanings. Then introduce the game by holding up two whales that are homonyms and one that belongs to a different pair. Ask the students to name the homonyms. Repeat until all the whale cards have been used.

4. Encourage the children to make new whale homonyms as they learn them. Store the whales in a file folder and place it in the classroom reading center. Encourage students to play the game during free time.

Simple Circle Games

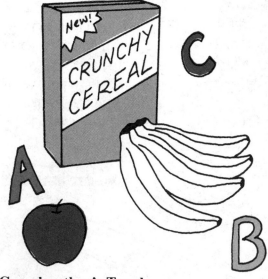

Grandmother's Trunk

1. Gather students in a circle. Give the class a theme with which to work, such as a trip or shopping in a food store. The leader begins by saying, "I went shopping and I bought cereal (or some other food product)." The next student must repeat what was said and add what he or she "bought" at the store as well. Continue until everyone has had a turn. Help the children who forget the sequence of objects bought.

2. Variations on this game are: give the class a specific letter with which the object must begin; ask the class to name objects in alphabetical order; have the class name objects that begin with the last letter of the object named in the previous turn.

Telephone

1. Ask students to sit in a tight circle. The leader says a word or phrase in the ear of the student sitting next to him or her.

2. That student then repeats the word or phrase into the ear of the student sitting next to him or her. This continues around the circle until the last student has heard it.

3. The last student announces the word or phrase. Have students compare whether or not what the last student says matches what the leader said. If it is different, ask the children to explain what happened.

Once upon a time there was an old house...

...It stood on the edge of a deep, dark wood...

...My friends and I didn't know who lived there...

Add to the Story

1. Gather students in a circle. The leader begins by starting a story with one or two sentences, such as, "One dark, rainy night, I decided to take a walk down by the river. I knew I would have to pass the old cemetery, but I went anyway." The next student in the circle adds another sentence or two to the story until the whole class has had a turn.

2. Recap the story sequence periodically for students. Remind the last few students that they need to make up the ending for the story. If students are enjoying their made-up story, let them continue for another round or two.

3. Tape record the story and play it back so students may hear it again. Then replay the story, stopping the tape randomly to ask the class to predict what will come next.

4. Invite volunteers to transcribe the story onto experience chart paper while other students draw pictures to illustrate. When students are ready, have them tape the pictures around the story.

Did I Say Something Wrong?

1. Read a favorite story to the class. Then explain that you will retell the story, but some parts will be different. If the children hear you say something wrong, they should raise their hands to point out the mistake.

2. Change names, places, or objects, or add new details in the retelling of the story. Make the story as hilarious or as tricky as you wish.

3. Play a variation of this game by pretending that you are a visitor to the class from another planet. Tell them about an adventure or a story about your visit to earth. For example, you may wish to say, "It was very hot the other day, so I made sure I wore my mittens and scarf." Encourage the students to say the sentences correctly, then repeat their corrections.

Figurative Speech Class Book

Materials:

- large sheet of paper
- crayons or markers
- 8 1/2" x 11" white paper
- construction paper
- hole puncher
- yarn

Directions:

1. Tape a large sheet of paper to a classroom wall or a bulletin board. Brainstorm with the class about the meaning of figurative speech. Provide students with an example, such as, "It's raining cats and dogs," and ask them to explain what it means. Then ask students to call out fanciful phrases they know while you write them on the paper.

2. Categorize the phrases with the class. For example, the phrase above would fit into a category about weather, or a category about animals.

3. Ask each student to choose a phrase he or she would like to illustrate. Have each student write the phrase on an 8 1/2" x 11" sheet of paper and draw a picture. Each student should then show his or her phrase to the class.

4. Make dividers by writing each category name on a different piece of construction paper. Insert the divider before the beginning of each category.

5. Punch holes in the left side of each page in the same position each time. Tie the pages together with yarn. If desired, share the book with other classes.

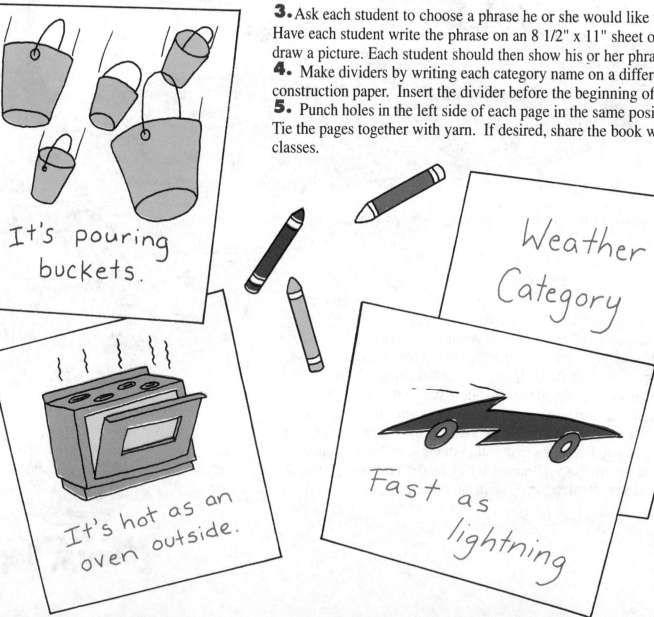

It's pouring buckets.

It's hot as an oven outside.

Weather Category

Fast as lightning

Books, Books, Books

Arrange a class field trip to the local library. Ask students to bring in their library cards for the trip. Several days before the trip, send home a note requesting permission to obtain library cards for those children who do not have them.

Ask the children's room librarian to help explain how a library works and what kinds of information can be obtained from the card catalog. Discuss the Dewey decimal system and how books are arranged alphabetically by author. If a computer is available, ask the librarian to show children how to use it to find the books they want.

After students are familiar with the organization, divide the class into small groups of three or four. Give each group several titles to locate in the children's room. Help students identify and solve any problems they have using the card catalog. If possible, read the book, *Check It Out! The Book About Libraries* by Gail Gibbons (published by Harcourt Brace Jovanovich, 1985), which describes how a library works.

After the field trip, challenge students to catalog the books in the classroom. Distribute the form on this page for students to record information about books they read at home and at school. Each week, ask several students to choose one of their books to share with the rest of the class.

Title: _____

Author: _____

Description: _____

_____

_____

_____

_____

Beginning Sounds Game

1. Divide the class into three groups. Ask each group to line up in front of the chalkboard.

2. Tell students that you are going to say a word. The first person in each line should go to the chalkboard and write down the beginning sound of that word.

3. The child who writes down the beginning sound first in each round scores a point for his or her team. Continue playing until each child has taken a turn. (You may wish to allow younger children to confer with their teammates before writing on the chalkboard.)

4. Extend the game by asking students to write down the ending or middle sound, spelling the entire word, writing the number of syllables in each word, or writing the opposite of the word.

In the Beginning

Solve this puzzle by circling the letter of the beginning sound of each animal.

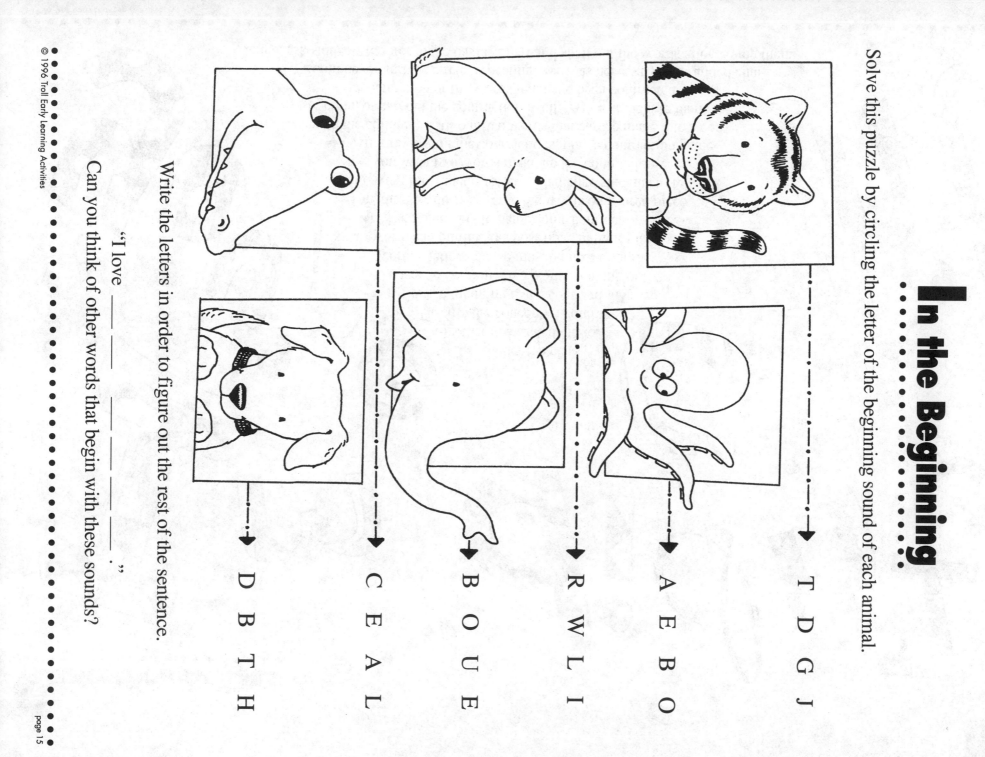

T D G J

A E B O

R W L I

B O U E

C E A L

D B T H

Write the letters in order to figure out the rest of the sentence.

"I love _____ _____ ."

Can you think of other words that begin with these sounds?

Contraction Actions

I'm didn't you're can't

1. Gather the class together in a seated circle. Discuss the concept of contractions, explaining that a contraction is a way to combine two words, leaving out certain letters and sounds to make a shorter word, and putting an apostrophe in their place.

2. Ask volunteers to name some contractions (i.e., I'm, didn't, you're). Write the words on a large piece of oaktag for students to see. Challenge students to tell you what two words make up the contractions.

3. After reviewing the contractions, play a contraction game with the children. Call out two words that can be made into a contraction, or call out the contraction itself. Ask a student to name the contraction or the words that have been contracted.

4. Continue around the circle, repeating words as necessary. For added challenge, ask students to refer to the oaktag chart and spell out the words after saying them.

Best Books for Early Readers

The whole language approach to reading incorporates predictable stories about topics that interest young children. These stories can often be turned into multifaceted lessons that build skills in a number of early learning areas.

Read some or all of the following stories to the class. Place the books in the reading center for students to look at during free time. Think of ways to extend these stories into other areas of learning, such as science experiments, history lessons, arts and crafts, and math projects.

Wagon Wheels by Barbara Brenner (HarperCollins, 1984)

Caps for Sale by Esphyr Slobodkina (HarperCollins, 1987)

Sylvester and the Magic Pebble by William Steig (Simon & Schuster, 1988)

What's That Noise? by Michele Lemieux (Morrow, 1985)

Loose Tooth by Steven Kroll (Scholastic, 1992)

Angelina and the Princess by Katharine Holabird (Crown, 1988)

Bill and Pete Go Down the Nile by Tomie de Paola (Putnam, 1987)

No Jumping on the Bed! by Tedd Arnold (Dial, 1987)

What Bounces? by Kate Duke (Dutton, 1986)

When We Went to the Park by Shirley Hughes (Lothrop Lee, 1985)

The Nutshell Library by Maurice Sendak (HarperCollins, 1962)

Is It the Same? Is It Different? Game

Materials:

- 9" x 12" construction paper
- crayons or markers
- file folder

Directions:

1. To make the playing cards, fold ten pieces of paper in half widthwise. Hold the papers with the fold at the top. Then draw a line down the middle from top to bottom.

2. In one half, draw a simple picture of a cup. In the other half, draw the cup with juice in it. On the inside, write the word "different."

3. On another piece of paper, draw a person's face in each half, making them identical. On the inside, write "same."

4. Some other suggestions are: a clock face showing 6 o'clock and a clock face showing 12 o'clock (different); a mug with a handle and a mug without a handle (different); mittens with the same pattern (same); an upper- and a lowercase A (different); fall tree/spring tree (different); two tulips (same); two windows with curtains (same).

different

same

5. Now introduce the game by holding up the first card so the class cannot see the inside. Ask students to look at the two pictures, then say if they are the same or different. Open the card for students to check their answer. As the children become more adept at the game, make more challenging cards, or let students create cards of their own.

6. Place the cards in a file folder for students to use during free time.

ord Games

Word Bingo

1. To make bingo cards, draw a line about 1″ from the top of a 5″ × 7″ index card, as shown. Then draw four columns, and write a 1 in the first column, a 2 in the second, a 3 in the third, and a 4 in the fourth. Draw four rows across the card, as shown. Then reproduce the card once for each student in the class or reading group.

2. In the first and second columns, write vocabulary words the students already know. In the third and fourth columns, write new vocabulary words. Vary the cards so there will be some different words appearing on each one.

1	2	3	4
funny	butter	gasoline	because
little	hello	building	heard
shout	read	thought	pumpkin
house	grow	sprinkle	balloon

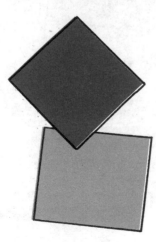

3. Make markers for the game by cutting out squares of construction paper.

4. Write the words on a master list in their proper columns. Call out the number column and a word at random. If a student has that word on the bingo card, he or she should place a marker over it. Continue until a student has all the words covered.

5. Play the bingo game with other configurations needed to win: a picture frame (around the perimeter of the bingo card); an ''H'' (two lines from top to bottom on both sides, a third line across the middle).

Word Games

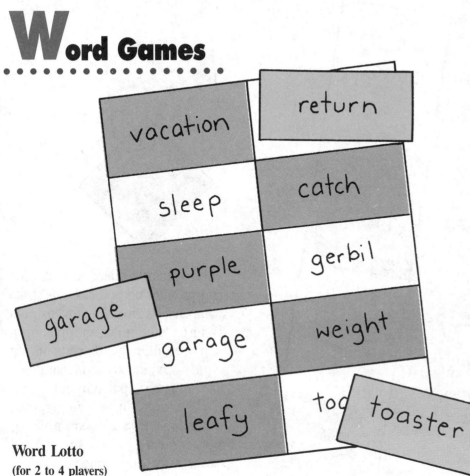

vacation

return

sleep

catch

purple

gerbil

garage

garage

weight

leafy

toaster

Word Lotto

(for 2 to 4 players)

1. Create game boards by dividing a 9" x 12" piece of paper into 10 boxes, as shown. Reproduce this paper four times.

2. In each box, write a word with which students are familiar or not familiar. Vary the words on each board.

3. Make small cards that are the same size as the boxes on the game boards. Write the words again on these cards.

4. Tell each player to choose a board. Call out one word at a time. Ask students to match each word card to the word on the board and lay the card down on that box. The first student to cover all the words on his or her board wins.

5. Vary the game by making pictures on either the board or the cards that students must match with words.

Word Concentration

(for two players)

1. On 2" x 2" cards, write words students are currently studying. Be sure each card has a double.

2. Lay the cards word-side down on a table. The first player chooses two cards and flips them over. If they match, he or she takes the cards and may take another turn. If the cards do not match, the player lays them word-side down again and the next player goes.

3. Continue the game until all cards have been paired. Players then count their pairs. The player with the most pairs wins.

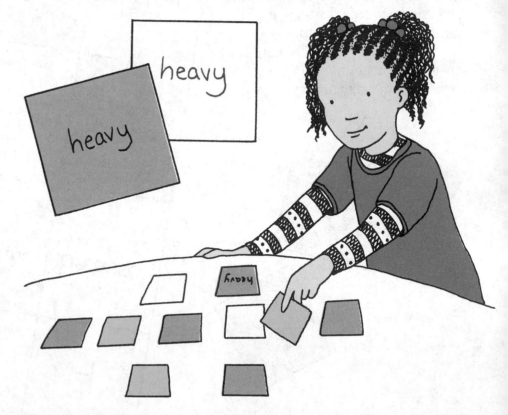

heavy

heavy

ord Charades

1. Write out simple nouns or action words on 5" x 7" index cards, one word per card. Choose words with which students are familiar, but vary the level of difficulty required to act out the word.

2. Divide the class into two teams. Have a member of one team stand, facing his or her team. Give that child a card.

sleeping

bird

3. The child may not use props, point, or speak while acting out the word. Whisper advice in his or her ear if necessary. As the student pantomimes the word, encourage group members to guess what it is. Give each group 1-2 minutes to guess the word, depending on the ages of the students playing the game.

4. Alternate play between teams. Each time a team guesses the word correctly within the time limit, that team scores a point.

5. Continue playing until everyone has had a chance to act out one word. The team with the most points at the end of the game wins.

Scrambled Sentences

3. Tell students to give the words to their partners. Challenge partners to reconstruct the sentences. (Remind students that there may be more than one way to make the words into a sentence.)

4. Have students switch roles and try again. Then ask students to take their cards with them as they change partners with their classmates.

5. Play the game once a week, encouraging students to increase the complexity of their sentences as they become more adept at reconstructing them.

1. Assign students partners to play this game. Have one child in each pair write out a sentence in large letters, leaving plenty of room between each word, as shown. Tell students to be sure that their partners cannot see the sentences as they write them.

2. Have the children cut apart the sentences into separate words.

Reading a Recipe

Materials:

- experience chart paper
- marker
- orange sherbet
- orange juice
- yogurt
- tablespoon
- blender
- cups

Directions:

1. Write the list below at the top of a large sheet of experience chart paper. Draw a simple picture next to each item so students can read the pictures if they cannot read the words.

orange sherbet

orange juice

yogurt

tablespoon

blender

cups

2. Write the following instructions on the paper for students to follow:

1. Measure two tablespoons each of orange sherbet, orange juice, and yogurt. Put them in a blender.
2. Turn the blender on and count to 10.
3. Turn the blender off.
4. Pour the shake into a cup and enjoy!

3. Read the instructions with students before they begin to make their shakes. Stand nearby to help students read the recipe and to make sure the blender is being used safely.

4. Discuss what they need to do first in order to make the recipe (gather the ingredients), what comes next (following the order of instructions), and what comes last (drinking the shake). Talk about what might have happened if students did not have all the ingredients, if they had used the wrong ingredients, or if they mixed up the order of the instructions.

Words Around Us

Materials:

- butcher paper
- crayons or markers
- scissors
- paint and paintbrushes
- 3" x 5" index cards
- tape

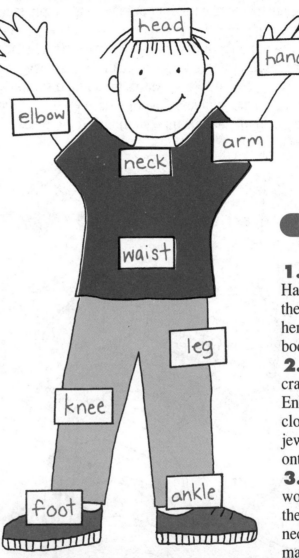

Directions:

1. Divide the class into pairs. Have one student lie down on the butcher paper while his or her partner traces around the body. Then switch roles.

2. Give students plenty of crayons, markers, and paint. Encourage students to draw clothes, hair, facial features, jewelry, and other features onto their tracings.

3. Ask volunteers to think of words that describe a part of the body (i.e., hand, fingers, neck). Instruct students to make a set of body-part words on 3" x 5" index cards.

4. Read over the cards with students and tape them in place on the body tracings.

5. Extend this activity by labeling the furniture, games, and toys in the room. Try switching a few words each day to see if students notice. If so, ask the children to reposition the word cards so they are all correct.

Graph This Story

1. Try this whole language approach to math. Begin by giving the class a short story or paragraph to read. When they are finished, ask them to make a graph of certain information found in the story or paragraph.

2. For example, reproduce the story below and ask students to read it, or read it for them.

One day, some children found an old treasure chest on the beach.

"Maybe it has jewels and gold in it," said Alex.

"Maybe it has a treasure map in it," said Rosie.

"Maybe it's the skeleton of a pirate who got trapped inside," said Maggie.

After opening it, they found seven goblets, three pearl necklaces, ten crowns, and five gold coins. There was also a letter that said the contents were the property of Old Peg Leg the Pirate, and if anyone touched his treasure chest they would be forced to walk the plank on his ship.

On the back of the letter was a map with a big X in the center. The friends began wondering if the map led the way to another treasure chest.

3. Graph the number of things found in the treasure chest. Draw lines for five columns on a large sheet of paper or oaktag, from top to bottom. Then write the word of each of the contents along the bottom, one in each column (goblets, necklaces, crowns, coins, letter).

4. Ask students to help draw 7 goblets, 3 necklaces, 10 crowns, 5 coins, and 1 letter to use for the graph. All the objects should be approximately the same size. Have students come to the graph and place their pictures above the correct words. Make sure the children do not leave large gaps between their pictures.

Goblets	Necklaces	Crowns	Coins	Letters
		👑		
		👑		
		👑		
🏆		👑		
🏆		👑		
🏆		👑	🪙	
🏆		👑	🪙	
🏆	📿	👑	🪙	
🏆	📿	👑	🪙	
🏆	📿	👑	🪙	✉️

5. Compare and contrast the amounts in each column. Ask questions, such as:

Which item did the treasure chest have the most of? (crowns)
Which column has the fewest items in it? (letters)
How many more necklaces were there than letters? (2)
How many fewer coins were there than goblets? (2)

6. Conclude by asking students to draw a picture of what they think the next treasure chest might contain. Make another graph and ask students to glue their pictures above the words that match their pictures. Ask similar questions to those above.

In a Hurry Word Cards

1. Write 30 current vocabulary words on 5" x 7" index cards, one word per card.

2. Explain to the class or reading group that they will see a word very quickly. They must read the word and say it aloud before it is flipped over. Play the game with one student at a time.

3. Hold a word card out to a student for a count of three, then flip it over so it cannot be seen. Ask the student to name the word. One point is given if the word is read correctly. Each student may mark his or her own points on a sheet of paper. Then repeat with the next student in the group.

4. The winner is the student who has the most points after all the words have been read.

5. For additional challenge, write words on the cards that have similar beginnings or endings. Students will need to look at the cards very carefully in order to tell them apart.

Parts of Speech Search

A **verb** is a word that shows action. A **noun** is a word that names a person, place, or thing. Circle all the verbs. Draw a rectangle around all the nouns. Are any of these words both nouns and verbs?

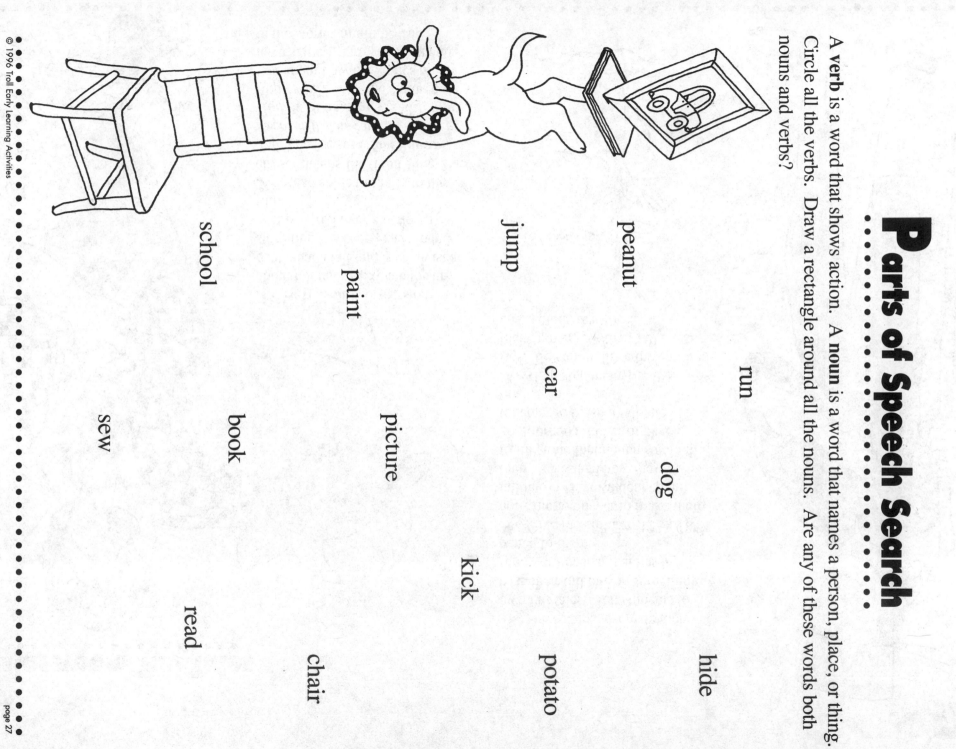

peanut

run

dog

hide

jump

car

picture

kick

potato

paint

book

chair

school

sew

read

Classroom Tall Tales

1. Have a class discussion about tall tales. Explain to students that a tall tale is an unusual story that has been exaggerated as it is retold over a period of time.

2. Read some tall tales to the class, such as the Troll First-Start® Tall Tales series (*Paul Bunyan*, *Pecos Bill*, *The Legend of Sleepy Hollow*, *John Henry*, and *Johnny Appleseed*). Ask the children to talk about how the stories might have started, and what elements in the stories might be true.

3. Have students create their own tall tales. Tell students to base their tall tale on something funny or unusual that has happened to them.

4. Give the children 12" x 18" construction paper to make their tall tales. Have students plan their stories and how they wish to illustrate them, then staple the appropriate number of pages together to make a tall tale big book.

5. Help students write their stories. Be sure to have the children make covers for their tall tales and include the titles.

Aesop's Fables Flannel Board Stories

The Lion and the Mouse

Long ago, a sleeping lion was awakened by a little mouse who accidentally ran over his paw. The lion, who was tired and grouchy, lost his temper and grabbed the little mouse.

"Why did you wake me up?" he roared. "Now I am going to eat you up!"

"Please don't!" cried the mouse. "I didn't mean to wake you up. If you let me go, I promise to repay your kindness someday."

The lion was amused that the little mouse thought that he could ever repay a favor to the king of the jungle. He laughed uproariously and let the mouse go free.

Several months later, the lion became trapped in a hunter's net. He roared with anger and tried to claw his way out, but to no avail. Just as he was about to give up, he heard a little voice calling him. It was the little mouse.

"I'll help you!" the mouse said, and he quickly began gnawing through the ropes of the net.

In no time at all, the mouse had set the lion free. The grateful lion thanked his little friend.

"I knew I would repay you," the mouse said, "for even the littlest creature can help the biggest creature."

The Fox and the Crow

One morning a crow was perched high up in a tree with a piece of cheese in her mouth. A clever fox happened by, and he decided to try to trick her into giving him the cheese.

The fox stopped under the tree and looked up at the crow admiringly. "I don't think I have ever seen a more magnificent-looking bird!" he said. "What beautiful feathers! What a noble beak!"

Then the fox sighed. "I doubt that her voice is as sweet as her looks, however, for then she would be the queen of all flying creatures."

The crow was feeling quite proud of herself, and she decided to show the fox that she did indeed have a wonderful voice. As she opened her beak, the cheese fell and tumbled into the fox's waiting mouth.

The fox gobbled the cheese and licked his lips as the crow looked on angrily. "You do have a nice voice after all," he said, "but it is far more important to have wits."

Aesop's Fables Flannel Board

Reproduce the figures below and on page 31. Color the figures and cut them out. Then glue a small piece of felt on the back of each figure to use on a flannel board. Encourage students to act out the stories using the figures, and to make up new stories of their own featuring these characters.

Aesop's Fables Flannel Board

Name _____

Math Words

Write out the number words for each numeral below.

27 _____

61 _____

99 _____

281 _____

362 _____

Now write out the numerals for these number words.

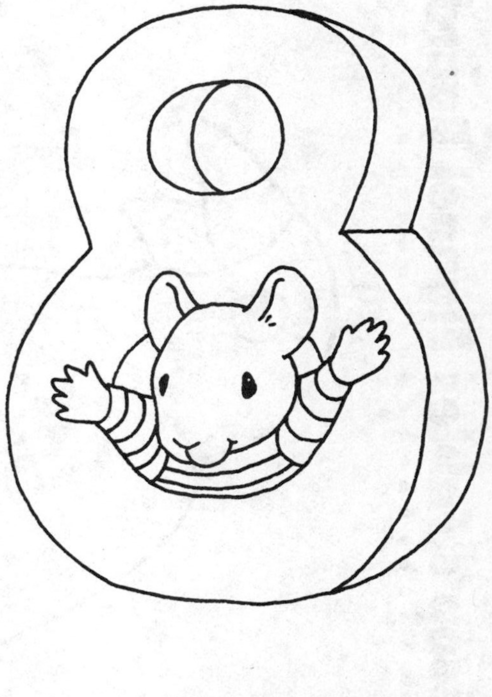

_____ **thirty-eight**

_____ **fifty-two**

_____ **eighty-seven**

_____ **one hundred six**

_____ **three hundred**

Mark Your Page

The Chalk Box Kid by Clyde R. Bulla (Random House, 1987)
Aunt Eater Loves a Mystery by Doug Cushman (HarperCollins, 1989)
Arthur's Loose Tooth by Lillian Hoban (HarperCollins, 1985)
Sarah, Plain and Tall by Patricia MacLachlan (HarperCollins, 1985)
Fox on the Job by James Marshall (Puffin, 1990)
Come Back, Amelia Bedelia by Peggy Parish (HarperCollins, 1971)
Junie B. Jones and the Stupid Smelly Bus by Barbara Park (Random House, 1992)
Marvin Redpost: Kidnapped at Birth? by Louis Sachar (Random House, 1992)
Oliver, Amanda, and Grandmother Pig by Jean Van Leeuwen (Dial, 1987)
Morris Goes to School by Bernard Wiseman (HarperCollins, 1970)

Materials:

- crayons or markers
- glue
- oaktag
- scissors

Directions:

1. Reproduce the bookmarks on page 34 for each student. Have students color the bookmarks, mount them on oaktag, and cut them out.
2. Ask the class why people use bookmarks (to hold their places in books). Discuss what a chapter book is, and why books are divided into chapters and scenes. Ask if anyone in the class has ever read a chapter book, or heard a chapter book read aloud. How is a chapter book different from a picture book?
3. Read some of the following chapter books with the class. Place the books in the reading center for students to look at during free time.

ark Your Page

Read *The Three Little Pigs* by yourself or with a friend. Then draw lines to match the pictures to their words.

Three Little Pigs Matching

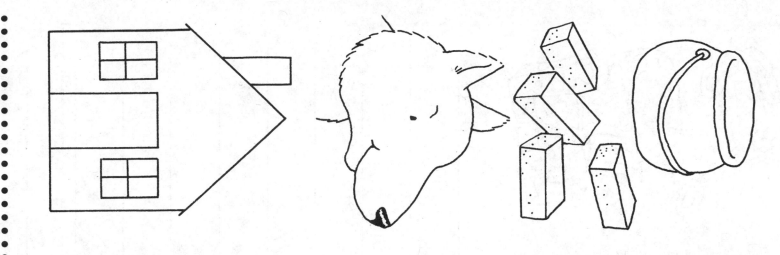

pig

wolf

house

straw

twigs

bricks

door

pot

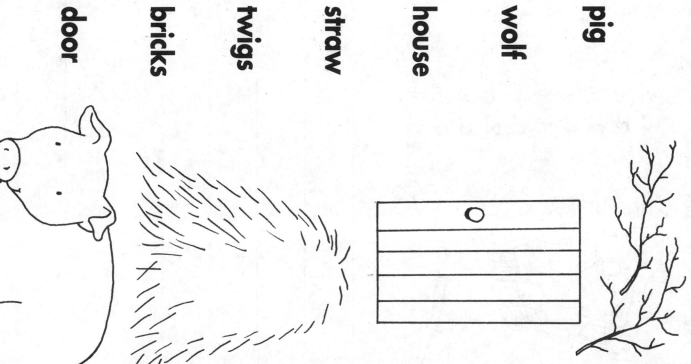

Mend the Blends

· · · · · · · · · · · · · · ·

The words below have been broken apart. See if you can make new words by matching each blend to one or more endings.

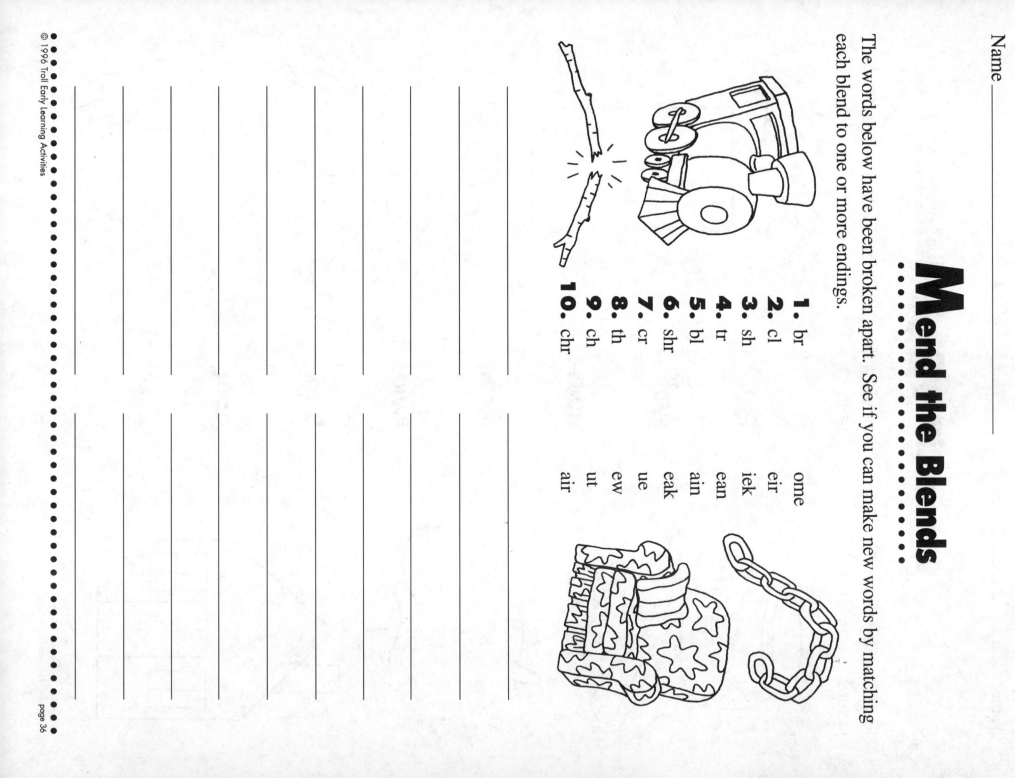

1.	br	ome
2.	cl	eir
3.	sh	iek
4.	tr	ean
5.	bl	ain
6.	shr	eak
7.	cr	ue
8.	th	ew
9.	ch	ut
10.	chr	air

© 1996 Troll Early Learning Activities

Punctuation Pen Pals

Write a letter to a pen pal. Use at least one of the punctuation marks below in each sentence.

What's Missing Here?

A thief has stolen all the punctuation marks from the sentences below! Write in the missing punctuation.

1. I bought apples bananas and carrots at the store

2. Do you want to go to the playground

3. Wow I can't believe my eyes

4. You are so funny she said

5. Are you on your way to school

Two Words in One

- crayons or markers
- construction paper
- scissors
- bright bulletin board paper
- stapler

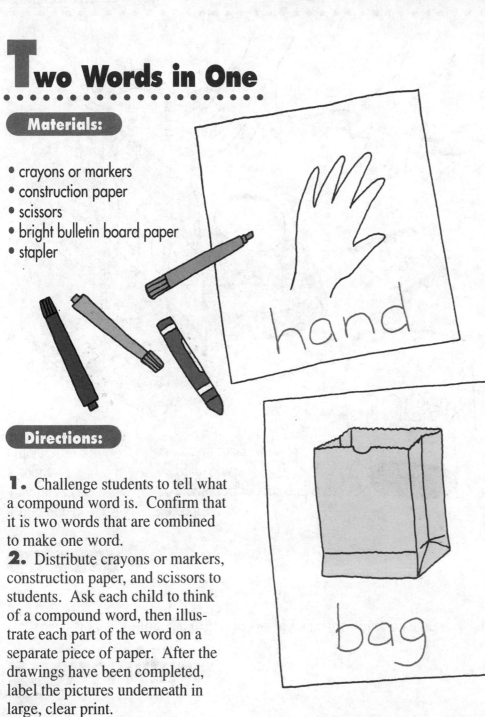

1. Challenge students to tell what a compound word is. Confirm that it is two words that are combined to make one word.

2. Distribute crayons or markers, construction paper, and scissors to students. Ask each child to think of a compound word, then illustrate each part of the word on a separate piece of paper. After the drawings have been completed, label the pictures underneath in large, clear print.

3. Staple bright paper to a bulletin board. Staple students' pictures onto the board randomly and write the following question: "How many compound words can you make from these words?"

4. Some suggestions for compound words to use: firefighter, mousetrap, downpour, handbag, cupcake, snapshot, lighthouse, bedroom, toothache, shipwreck, football, clubhouse, flashlight, and raincoat. Try to use compound words whose parts are found in other compound words.

retzel Initials

Help each student follow the recipe below to make his or her own pretzel initials.

Materials:

- package of yeast
- warm water
- sugar
- flour
- beaten egg
- coarse salt
- measuring spoons and cups
- small bowls
- cookie sheet

Directions:

1. Measure 3 tablespoons of warm water into a small bowl.

2. Sprinkle 1/2 teaspoon of yeast into the water. Stir until the yeast dissolves.

3. Mix in 1/2 teaspoon of sugar and 1/2 cup of flour.

4. Knead for several minutes.

5. Divide the dough into two to four pieces. Roll the pieces into worms. Then shape them into letters, pinching the dough together where the letters intersect. Place the letters on a cookie sheet.

6. Brush the initials with some of the beaten egg. Sprinkle with coarse salt.

7. Bake at 425°F for 15 minutes. Let cool, then serve as a snack.

Our Favorite Quilt

Read *The Josefina Story Quilt* by Eleanor Coerr (HarperCollins, 1986) to the class. After discussing the story, extend the lesson with this whole language activity.

Materials:

- 8" x 8" squares of muslin
- fabric markers or paint
- paintbrushes
- glue/fusing tape/needle and thread

Directions:

1. Give each student a square of muslin cloth. Ask each student to think about his or her favorite thing in the world. It could be a toy, a book, a food, music, or anything he or she wishes.

2. Using fabric markers or paint, ask each student to draw his or her favorite thing onto the square. Caution students to leave a 1" border of material around the edges of their drawing for sewing. Ask the children to sign their work when they are done.

3. When all the squares have been completed, check to see that they form a larger square or rectangle. If the rectangle is incomplete, ask some other people in the school, such as the principal, nurse, custodian, or librarian, to contribute to the quilt.

4. To attach the squares with a sewing machine, sew along a 1/2" seam allowance, turning under the edges when done to make a 1/2" hem. To attach the squares with glue, lay the quilt out by overlapping the edges of the squares by 1/2". Glue the edges together and trim the outer edges when done.

5. Hang the quilt in a school hallway or a display case for all to enjoy.

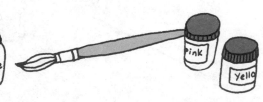

Mailbox Center

Materials:

- boxes with interior dividers
- crayons or markers
- construction paper
- scissors
- glue

Directions:

1. Collect boxes with interior dividers, making sure you have one divider space for each child. Let students use crayons or markers to decorate the outside of the boxes with pictures. Encourage children to use construction paper, scissors, and glue to make cut-out figures and designs for their boxes as well.

2. Ask each student to make a nameplate to glue on the top of his or her divider in the mailbox. Make the nameplates about 3″ high, and as wide as the divider spaces allow. Fold over 1″ at the top and glue to the top of each divided space so it hangs down into each student's assigned box.

3. Allow students to write or draw pictures to each other during free time. When a letter has been completed, that child may go to the mail center and place it in the appropriate box. Remind students to address the letters and sign their names.

4. Set aside ten minutes at the end of the day and assign a mail carrier to the mail center. The mail carrier may take the letters from the box and deliver them to the students. Or, students may look in their boxes for mail as they leave the room at the end of the day.

5. If desired, assign a new pen pal for each day to ensure that each student receives a letter, and to vary the content of students' writings.

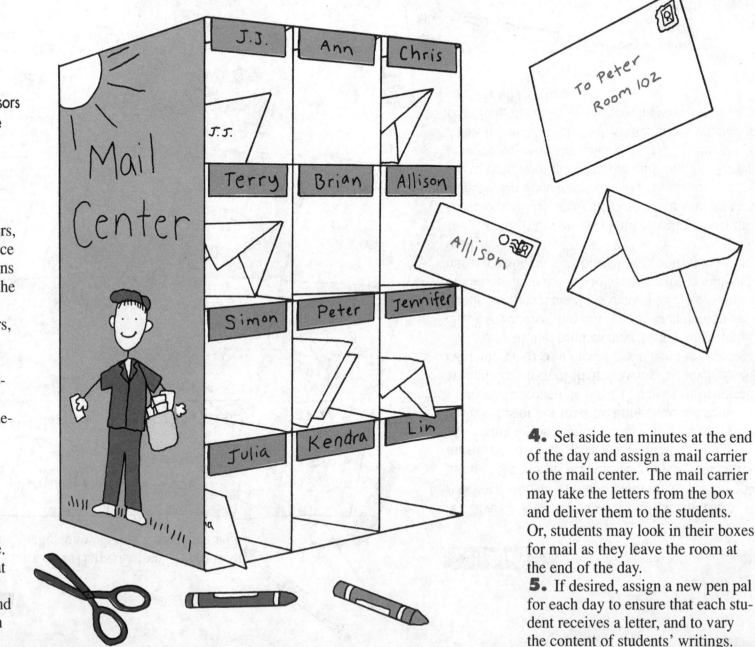

Writing Center

Materials:

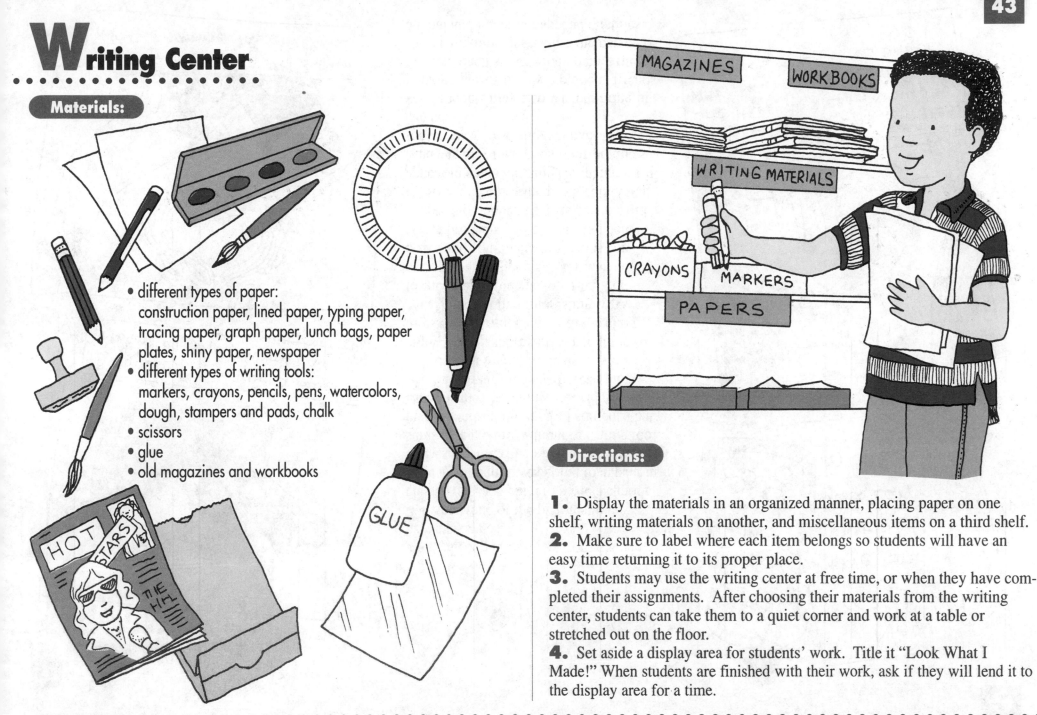

- different types of paper:
  construction paper, lined paper, typing paper,
  tracing paper, graph paper, lunch bags, paper
  plates, shiny paper, newspaper
- different types of writing tools:
  markers, crayons, pencils, pens, watercolors,
  dough, stampers and pads, chalk
- scissors
- glue
- old magazines and workbooks

MAGAZINES   WORKBOOKS

WRITING MATERIALS

CRAYONS   MARKERS

PAPERS

Directions:

1. Display the materials in an organized manner, placing paper on one shelf, writing materials on another, and miscellaneous items on a third shelf.
2. Make sure to label where each item belongs so students will have an easy time returning it to its proper place.
3. Students may use the writing center at free time, or when they have completed their assignments. After choosing their materials from the writing center, students can take them to a quiet corner and work at a table or stretched out on the floor.
4. Set aside a display area for students' work. Title it "Look What I Made!" When students are finished with their work, ask if they will lend it to the display area for a time.

Picture Writing

Bessie the pig won a blue ribbon at the county fair.

Tina Trutone sang the anthem at the game last weekend.

1. Collect photographs from old and new magazines.

2. Show one of the pictures to the class. Ask each child to write a caption for it as though it was going to appear in a newspaper. Explain that a caption sums up a picture without revealing too many details about it. Tell students that captions may be funny or serious.

3. Encourage students to read their captions out loud. Students may also enjoy writing short stories about the pictures and sharing them with the class.

4. Think of other interesting ways to encourage students to write. For example, ask students to bring in empty boxes and containers of various consumer products. Allow each student to choose a product. Then ask each child to write a label for the product that will appear in an advertising campaign for it. Students may then pitch their products for the class to see how persuasive they can be.

5. Students may also wish to bring in photographs of family members, friends, or pets. Each student may then write a short paragraph describing the person or animal and his or her special qualities.

NEW
CRAZY BUBBLES

New Crazy Bubbles, the most FUN you can have in the tub!

My cat's name is Jingles. She likes to sleep in my lap. When my friends come over, she runs and hides under the couch.

Recommended Reading

SHHH... Reading Zone

OUR BOOK REVIEWS
mrs. Smith's Class—Rm. 102

1. Reproduce the review sheet on page 46 five times for each student.

2. Have students place the review sheets in their file folders. After a child has finished a book he or she has particularly enjoyed, ask that student to fill out one of the review forms. Students may also enjoy coloring the review form.

3. Leave a file box in the reading center in which students may place their reviews.

4. After each student has filled out all five reviews, gather the class together to read through the reviews. Categorize the different types of books, and place duplicate reviews of titles together.

5. Punch holes along the left sides of the reviews. Bind them together with yarn, as shown. Place the reviews in the classroom library for students to refer to when choosing books.

Name ____________________

Recommended Reading

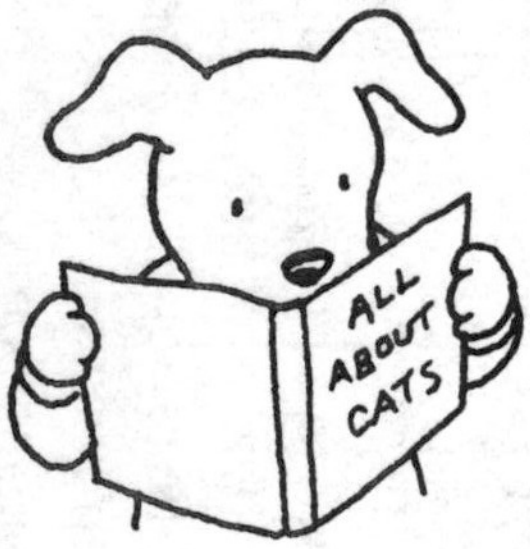

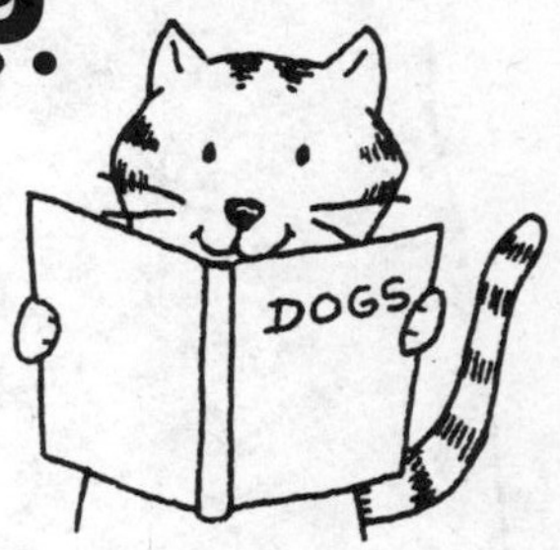

☆ Title: ____________________

☆ Author: ____________________

☆ Plot: ____________________

☆ Characters: ____________________

☆ I would recommend this book because:

Making a Class Big Book

Materials:

- 15" x 18" piece of bulletin board paper
- 8" x 14" cardboard pieces
- glue
- 12" x 18" white or manila paper
- needle and thread
- masking tape
- crayons or markers

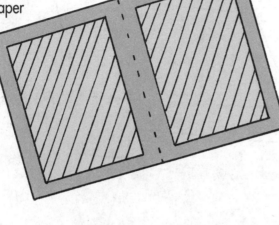

Directions:

1. Lay a piece of 15" x 18" bulletin board paper flat on a table. Fold it in half widthwise, then open the paper again. Center an 8" x 14" piece of cardboard in each half.

2. Glue the cardboard pieces down. Turn in the corners of the paper and glue them onto the cardboard, as shown. Then fold in all the edges of the bulletin board paper and glue onto the cardboard.

3. Fold 15 sheets of white or manila drawing paper in half, then open again. Center the sheets over the center of the cover.

4. Using a needle and thread, sew down the center of the book, as shown.

5. Wrap masking tape over the center of the book, inside and out, to cover the thread and help hold it in place.

6. Glue the first page to the inside front cover and the last page to the inside back cover.

7. Select a book to read to the class that is suitable for extension activities, such as *Can I Keep Him?* by Steven Kellogg (Dial, 1971). When the story is finished, ask students to name some other animals that they could bring home as a pet and what might happen if they did. (For example, if they brought home a seal, it would stay in the tub for hours and no one could take a bath.)

8. Ask the class to brainstorm to come up with a story for a class book. Write the title of the book on the first page. Place the book in the writing center.

9. Assign part of the story to each student. Have each child write and illustrate his or her part of the story.

10. When all the children have completed their assignments, have volunteers design and decorate a cover for the book. Be sure to write the title on the cover.

11. Read the book to the class, then leave it on display on a bookshelf so students may read it, or share it with another class during quiet time.

Riddle Mini-Book

Materials:

- 5" x 7" index cards
- crayons or markers
- large sheet of oaktag
- glue

Directions:

1. Fold an index card in half. On the front flap, write a riddle. On the inside, write the answer. The riddles may be difficult, silly, or simple. They should only be about three or four lines long. Be sure students give sufficient clues.

2. Fold a large sheet of oaktag in half. Glue the riddle cards to the inside of the oaktag. Place the cards in rows, or randomly around the oaktag.

3. Ask volunteers to decorate the cover of the oaktag. Leave the riddles on a bookshelf in the reading center for students to look at during free time.

When raindrops fall, I go up. What am I?

An umbrella

Our Riddle Book

My Own Dictionary

A
appreciate
antelope
angle
angel

B
bumblebee
bicycle
become
bubble

My Own Dictionary

C
caterpillar
captain
ceiling

D
difficult
daffodil

1. Help students develop more confidence in their spelling skills by creating their own dictionaries. Reproduce the cover on page 50 once for each child. Have children color the cover and mount it on sturdy construction paper.
2. Give each child 26 pieces of writing paper. Have children staple these pages together, along with another piece of sturdy construction paper to use as the back cover.
3. Instruct students to write the letter "A" on the first page of each book. Write the letter "B" on the next page, and so on.
4. When a student asks how to spell a certain word, tell him or her the correct spelling and ask the child to record the word in the dictionary under the letter of its beginning sound. The next time the child wants to know how to spell that word, he or she can look up the correct spelling in the dictionary.
5. Encourage students to continually add words to their dictionaries. As their ability to look up words increases, introduce students to a first dictionary as a source for spelling and definition questions.

© 1996 Troll Early Learning Activities

Name _____

My Own Dictionary

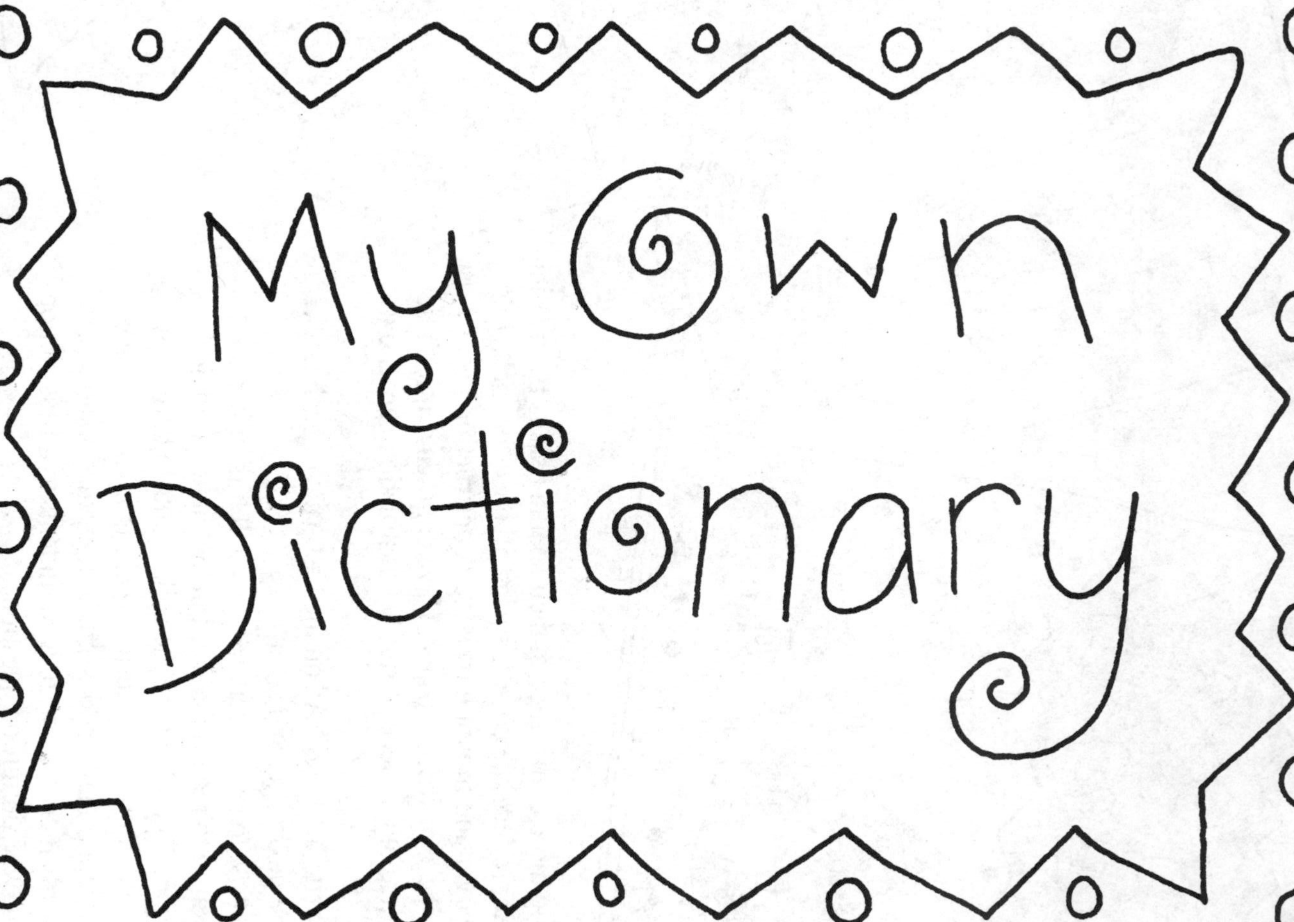

My Own Dictionary

Monthly Words

Each month, gather the class together to create a monthly thematic word list. Write the name of the month at the top of a large piece of paper. Tape the paper to an easel.

Ask volunteers to think of words that represent the featured month. Students may suggest words that relate to holidays, seasonal words, or words that represent school activities.

Display each word list for the entire month. Play games that utilize the words on the list. For example, younger students might enjoy categorizing the words on the list according to their beginning sound or part of speech. For older children, use the word list to make up vocabulary tests, short stories, poems, or word games (such as crossword puzzles and word finds).

APRIL

spring
rainy
daffodils
tulips
umbrellas
puddles
Easter
Passover

bunnies
eggs
mat
hap
gr
s
lavender
softball

OCTOBER

autumn   sweaters
harvest   chilly
pumpkins   raking
apples   leaves
cider   red
Halloween   yellow
ghosts   orange
witches   brown

Name _____

Parts of Speech
....

Fill in the blanks in the sentences below using words from the box. Then write the part of speech underneath each word. The first sentence has been done for you.

reading	teacher	little	red
rich	kicked	ball	store

1. I went to the ___store___ after school.
         noun

2. How old is your _____ brother?

3. My dog likes to catch a _____ .

4. I _____ a 20-yard field goal!

5. Who is your _____ for science class?

6. Her car is a large, _____ minivan.

7. I just finished _____ that book last night.

8. The prince was so _____ , he had stacks of gold all over the castle.

Name _____

We're Learning
....

Add an "ing" ending to these action words.

1. read _____

2. throw _____

3. go _____

4. help _____

5. toss _____

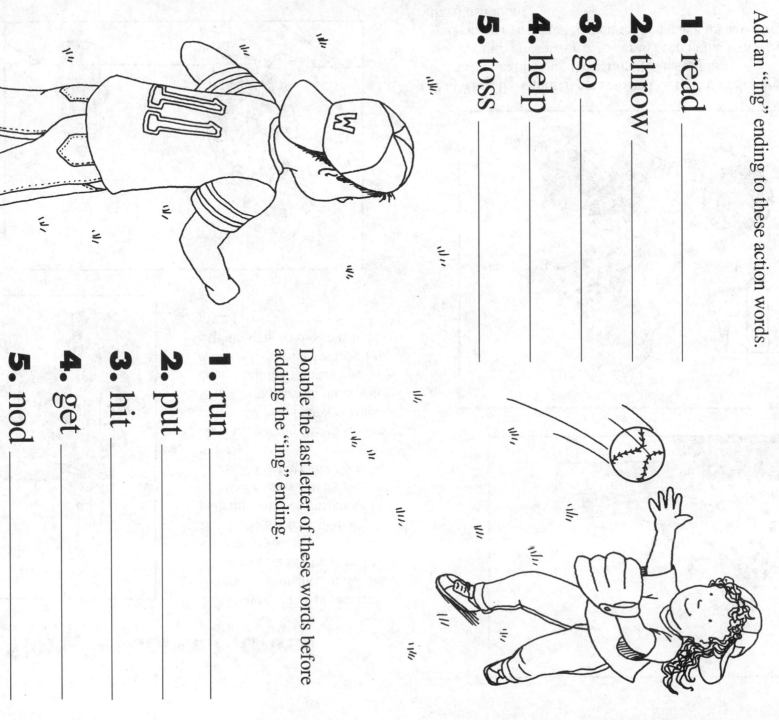

Double the last letter of these words before adding the "ing" ending.

1. run _____

2. put _____

3. hit _____

4. get _____

5. nod _____

Tell a Story Sequence Pictures

1. Draw a series of pictures showing a sequence of events. The series should be three to six pictures long.

2. Place the series on a bulletin board or chalkboard where the class can easily see them. Do not arrange them in order.

3. Ask a volunteer to find the first picture and put it on the left. Continue with other students until the sequence is arranged. Ask each student to explain why he or she is moving a picture.

4. When the children are satisfied that the pictures are in order, ask them to tell a story explaining the action that takes place.

5. Put the series in a file folder to keep in the writing center. Encourage students to rearrange the pictures and make up new stories to go along with the illustrations.

Finish the Story

1. Read aloud a story with which the class is not familiar. Pause before reading the ending and close the book.

2. Ask students to create their own endings for the story. If necessary, recap the sequence of events for students. Provide students with paper and crayons or markers to use to write and illustrate their endings.

3. When students have had a chance to predict the story's outcome, read the ending to them. Then ask volunteers to share their endings with the class.

4. Compare and contrast the endings students gave with the author's ending. Discuss which they liked better. Ask volunteers to describe what they think the characteristics of a good ending are.

Mr. Rabbit thinks he has time for a nap because he can easily win the race against such a slowpoke. Mr. Turtle crawls right by the sleeping bunny and wins!

Mr. Rabbit is faster, so he wins the race. He throws a party and shares his prize, a giant carrot, with Mr. Turtle.

Dialogue Pictures

3. Ask students to have a conversation based upon the clues in the picture. Encourage students to incorporate the surroundings, objects, facial expressions, or clothes the subjects in the picture might be wearing.

4. Vary the pictures to convey different feelings to the students: anger, happiness, sadness, surprise, disgust, love.

5. Ask students to write the dialogues they have created. Each child may write a sentence or two in a speech or thought balloon and attach it to the people or animals in the pictures.

1. Cut pictures from magazines that show two or more people (or animals) in conversation with each other, or simply positioned near each other.

2. Show one picture to the group. Choose two students to come forward and pretend to be one of the pictured people or animals.

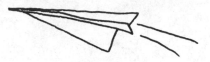

Show-and-Tell Speeches

1. Ask students to think up a favorite hobby, sport, pet, or talent, and invite them to give short speeches to the class about their favorite things.

2. Allow 15 minutes for students to prepare their speeches. For example, if a student likes bicycles, he or she may choose to explain how to change a flat tire. Another student may choose to explain how to play a video game.

3. Help students break down the instructions so they are clear to children who know nothing about the topic.

4. Give each student time to complete his or her speech at home if necessary. Limit the speeches to two minutes each. Encourage students to ask questions about any aspect of each speech.

Mystery Box

© 1996 Troll Early Learning Activities

Materials:

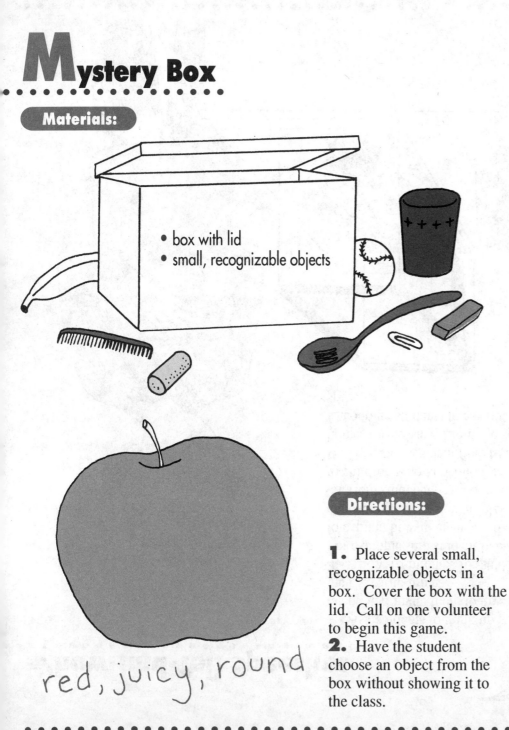

- box with lid
- small, recognizable objects

red, juicy, round

Directions:

1. Place several small, recognizable objects in a box. Cover the box with the lid. Call on one volunteer to begin this game.
2. Have the student choose an object from the box without showing it to the class.

3. Ask the student to give three adjectives that describe the chosen object. The student then chooses a volunteer who thinks he or she knows what the object is. If that child guesses correctly, the object is brought out for all to see and he or she takes the next turn. If the guess is incorrect, the student chooses another classmate to guess what the object is.
4. Continue the game until all objects have been named. You can substitute new objects and play the game at another time.

long, yellow, wooden

hard, smelly, rectangular

soap

The Misunderstood Skunk

Materials:

- crayons or markers
- scissors
- black and white yarn pieces
- oaktag
- lunch bags
- glue

Directions:

1. Reproduce the skunk patterns on pages 60–61 once for each child. Have students color the patterns and cut them out.

2. To make the tail, students may wish to glue black yarn along the edges and white yarn on the inner section. Have students mount the tail on oaktag to provide strength.

3. Glue the head to the bottom of the lunch bag. Glue the body so the bottom of the head meets the top of the body.

4. Add the arms, legs, and bow tie to the skunk, as shown. Then glue the tail to the back of the bag to complete the puppet.

5. Show the children how to make the skunk move by sliding their hands into the bags and curling their fingers into the folded bottoms.

6. Teach the class the following poem to act out with their skunk puppets.

Woe is me!
I've done it again.
And just when I thought
I'd found a true friend.

I saw her there
At the edge of the wood.
I was so thrilled,
I felt so good.

But as soon as she saw
My black-and-white tail,
Away she ran,
All frightened and pale.

What can it be
That makes them all run?
I'm only a skunk
Who wants to have fun!

7. Conclude by having students write their own adventures about the misunderstood skunk.

The Misunderstood Skunk

The Misunderstood Skunk

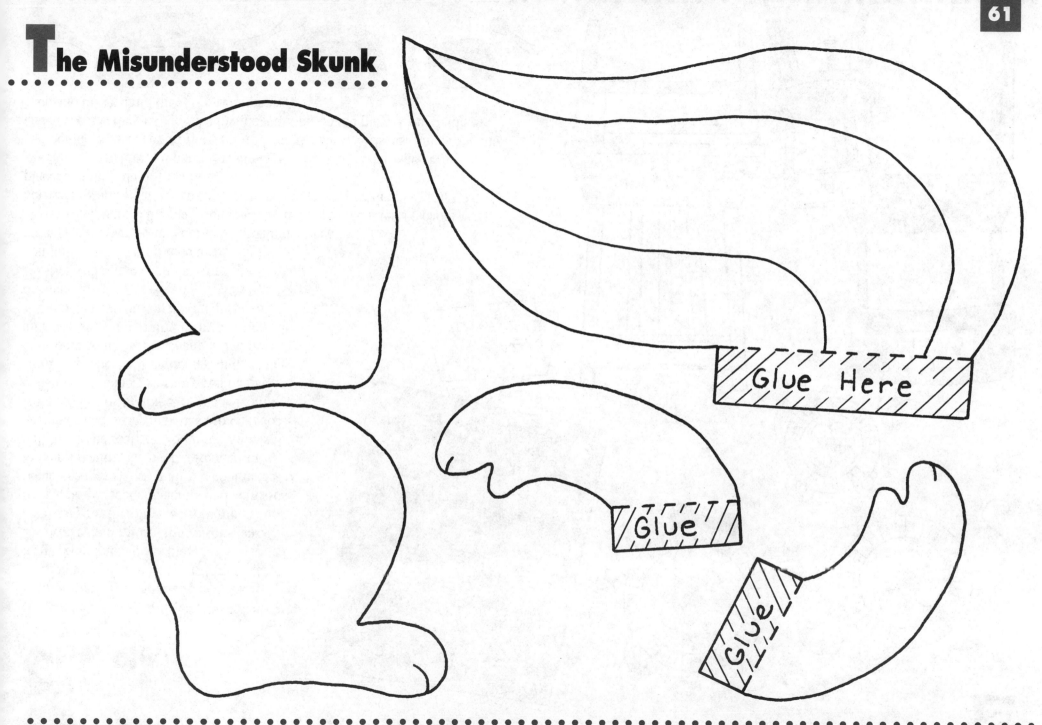

Glue Here

Glue

Glue

Class Play

1. Choose a story with which students are familiar for them to dramatize. Ask for nominations, then vote on a story suitable for making into a class play.

2. Make committees for various tasks necessary for the play: scriptwriters, costumes, props, scenery, actors and actresses, scene changes. Work with the committees to help organize their jobs. Remind the children to be realistic about their goals: costumes and props may have to be made from clothes from home, or made from construction paper; scenery can be made from large sheets of cardboard and oaktag and some paint; scene changes can be announced by a narrator, or by writing Scene 1 (and so on) on a large piece of oaktag.

3. Set aside time each day for each committee's work and rehearsals. Enlist parents and other volunteers to help with the play.

4. A week before the play, send out invitations to the guests (school workers, parents and relatives) telling them when and where the play will take place, and the title of the play.

5. The day before, prepare refreshments to be ready when the performers and behind-the-scenes workers return from the show. Discuss any problems and successes they experienced while working on the play. Congratulate each and every child on a job well done!

Name _____

On With the Show

Mrs. Sillystuff's class is putting on a play. Circle the ten things wrong with this picture.

SCRIPT

DIRECTOR

SCRIPT

Answers

page 15

"I love to read."

page 27

Verbs: run, hide, jump, kick, paint, read, sew
Nouns: dog, peanut, car, potato, picture, school, book, chair
Both nouns and verbs: hide, paint, book

page 32

twenty-seven	38
sixty-one	52
ninety-nine	87
two hundred eighty-one	106
three hundred sixty-two	300

page 35

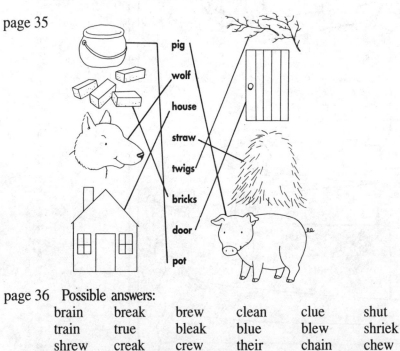

page 36   Possible answers:

brain	break	brew	clean	clue	shut	chrome
train	true	bleak	blue	blew	shriek	chair
shrew	creak	crew	their	chain	chew	

page 38

1. I bought apples, bananas, and carrots at the store.
2. Do you want to go to the playground?
3. Wow! I can't believe my eyes.
4. "You are so funny," she said.
5. Are you on your way to school?

page 52

1. I went to the <u>store</u> after school. (noun)
2. How old is your <u>little</u> brother? (adjective)
3. My dog likes to catch a <u>ball</u>. (noun)
4. I <u>kicked</u> a 20-yard field goal! (verb)
5. Who is your <u>teacher</u> for science class? (noun)
6. Her car is a large, <u>red</u> minivan. (adjective)
7. I just finished <u>reading</u> that book last night. (verb)
8. The prince was so <u>rich</u>, he had stacks of gold all over the castle.
(adjective)

page 53

1. reading   1. running
2. throwing   2. putting
3. going   3. hitting
4. helping   4. getting
5. tossing   5. nodding

page 63

1. The word "DIRECTOR" is upside down on the chair.
2. Handles are mismatched on hutch drawers.
3. There is a sneaker on the top shelf of the hutch.
4. The boy's hat is upside down.
5. The boy is missing his left shoe.
6. Ice-cream cone is on the stage.
7. The boy has a tail.
8. The girl is wearing roller skates.
9. It's sunny outside one window, but raining outside the other.
10. The girl is wearing a mitten on her left hand.